Fall Forward

Fall Forward

Your Purpose Is Waiting for You

Dr. Regina Banks-Hall

RBH Professional Publishing
Southfield, Michigan

Fall Forward
Copyright © 2016, 2019 Dr. Regina Banks-Hall
All rights reserved.
No part of this book may be used or reproduced in any manner whatsoever without written permission in writing from the publisher.

Published by:
RBH Professional Publishing, a division of
RBH Professional Development Institute, LLC
Southfield, MI 48075
www.rbankshall.com

Scripture taken from the Holy Bible New International Version, NIV, Copyright ©1973, 1978, 1984 International Bible Society. Used by permission of Zondervan Publishing House.

Scripture taken from the New King James Version (NKJV) ®, Copyright © 1982 by Thomas Nelson, Inc. Used by permission. All rights reserved

Scripture taken from the King James Version (KJV)

First edition published by Professional Woman Publishing 2016

Library of Congress Cataloging-in-Publication Data
Library of Congress Control Number:2019908826

ISBN: 978-1-7339533-0-6
eISBN: 978-1-7339533-1-3

Dedication

This book is dedicated to my parents, Bishop Jake and First Lady, Estella Burgess. Thank you for your love and support throughout my entire life. This book is also dedicated to my husband, Dolphus F. Hall Jr. Thank you for encouraging me to follow my dreams and explore new paths and opportunities. And lastly, this book is dedicated to anyone who has ever fallen. My prayer is that this book will be your hand up, and your push, as you fall forward into your purpose.

Contents

Introduction ix

ONE - Take Control and Begin the Journey 1

TWO - Forgive Yourself and Learn from Your Mistakes 7

THREE - Define Your Value – What are you Worth? 13

FOUR - Find your Passion 25

FIVE - Change your mindset with Positive Affirmations 29

SIX - Embrace Life - Mind, Body, & Spirit 35

SEVEN - You are a Virtuous Woman 41

About the Author 49

Introduction

Hello everyone, what you hold in your hands is a part of my journey. It represents how I overcame my fear, and began to walk into my destiny and purpose. As I reflect over my life, my journey was filled with setbacks, disappointments, heartaches and adversity. However, through it all, I concluded that I was an ordinary woman, capable of doing extraordinary things. This book is designed to help you overcome struggles with fear, rejection, depression, and emotional insecurities. Once free, it will provide a pathway for you to rise from your ordinary existence and enter into your extraordinary destiny and purpose.

I grew up during the 1970s when women, minorities and other marginalized people were fighting to find their place in America. The world was struggling to hold onto traditional roles for women, as women began to express their desire for more. During this time, my parents became ministers, and I spent the latter part of the seventies raising my brothers and sisters.

It was during this time that I noticed that television shows such as the Mary Tyler Moore Show, Maude, All in the Family, Alice, and One Day at a Time, all showed a variety of roles for women, right in the midst of this power struggle for traditional roles. As a minority, I looked at television shows such as Good Times, which identified the struggle of minorities, and the Jefferson's, which represented hope and upward mobility. In general, these shows brought attention to the climate of the country at that time.

As a child, I questioned everything and always looked for an answer to a question that perplexed me. Why some of us were born to struggle and others seemed destined for prosperity and success? I was also pushing back on church rules at that time. I believed that these rules, which were usually "man-made," not biblical, and steeped in tradition, limited my freedom and creativity.

These rules were mainly designed for women, and represented barriers to success. Unfortunately, these questions and struggles would haunt me my entire childhood.

Thankfully, my parents would enroll me in Cass Technical High School, and it was there I learned that all people mattered. Cass Tech was full of young students of many races, creeds and colors, bringing with them a wealth of culture and experiences. The school also provided a culture for "free thinkers" and encouraged every student to strive for excellence. At Cass Tech, being different was the norm and not the exception. It was here that I learned that it was okay to become my own person, strive for excellence and embrace my individuality.

I would continue on my quest for knowledge, and an answer to my perplexing question. I graduated from high school and began working and thinking about the future. I met my husband, we married, and I thought my life was now complete. However, although I was happily married, I knew something was missing from my life. I just did not know what it was. I set out on a quest to find myself. During this quest, I would sell cosmetics, start a Corporation, and continued the pursuit of my purpose.

As I continued on my journey, I would meet many women who struggled with fear, depression, abuse, etc. Regardless of our professions, credentials or possessions, in our own private moments, we each are holding the same conversation. How can I overcome this mountain? Should I lose weight? Is my hair the right color? Do I have enough education? Am I qualified for the position?

Fear, insecurity, and doubt among women is vast. It haunts us, but we can overcome. Part of the journey is realizing the problem and being willing to face it head on. It is also important to note, that we hold ourselves back by lacking self-confidence, pulling back, lowering our expectations, and settling for second best. By settling, we limit our ability to strive for first place, and possibly, expand the misconception that we do not belong.

My journey inspired a desire for higher education. I had no idea that through this desire, I would realize that my destiny and purpose was to inspire others to follow their dreams and passions. As I began to think about writing this book, I began to focus on what makes us feel insecure. Why are we afraid? What holds us back from following our dreams? How can we as ordinary people, do something extraordinary? What I have realized through my own journey is that we have to find courage, face our fears, and believe that our mission is worth the challenge.

As you read these chapters, focus on what you want to achieve out of life and identify your purpose. Let go of the fear, and know that the mission is not about you, but about the lives you will transform when you achieve your goals.

ONE
Take Control and Begin the Journey

"I am here to change the world with small acts of kindnesses, realizing that my small attempt to empower everyone supports the greater good"
— Dr. Regina Banks-Hall

It was a cold November night in 2008. I was at home washing a turkey getting ready for my Thanksgiving dinner and the telephone rang. It was Kelly Automotive Services, calling to inform me that my contract assignment with the Chrysler Corporation was ending. I hung up the phone, shared the news with my husband, and went back into the kitchen. The following Monday, I would file for unemployment for the first time in 25 years. Over the next few weeks, the shock would turn into anger. I could not believe I was unemployed. I survived Thanksgiving and Christmas, and began the New Year with the reality of collecting unemployment insurance.

For several months, I would get up, make myself a cup of coffee, and climb back in my bed. One day while watching television, I realized that God had given me a second chance for success. However, to embrace the opportunity, I had to end my pity party and get out of the bed. I focused on my favorite scripture, which states, "I can do all things through Christ who strengthens me" (Philippians 4.13). A few weeks later, I received a letter to attend a meeting regarding a program helping individuals interested in finishing their education, or earning an advanced degree. I learned that I qualified for this program and prepared to go back to school. Within two short years, and a lot of hard work, I would earn my MBA Degree. With momentum building and a new outlook on life, I would then set my sights on a Doctorate Degree in Business Administration.

During this period of personal development, I also focused on generating some new experiences. As I began settling into my new life, I started to find a purpose in what I was doing. I was working as a substitute teacher, volunteering time as a budget counselor for my church, and continued my quest for higher levels of education. I was also helping my family by attending to the needs of my father-in-law who was ill. I was beginning to see a future for myself, and finding joy in how God was using my gifts and talents.

One day while I was working in an elementary school, breaking up a fight, I felt the vibration of my cell phone. After checking the message, someone was calling me with a job offer. I jumped at the opportunity and three years later, I would become the Manager of that department. As I began to make changes personally, I began to grow and develop as an individual. Now, as I evaluate the last eight years, optimism, passion, finding my inner strength, and taking control of my life were the keys to success.

Today, I am a Professor, with a Doctorate Degree in Leadership, the President of RBH Professional Development Institute, an International author and co-author of six books, a blogger, and host of my own YouTube channel. I am also a certified motivational speaker, business trainer, and life coach, encouraging others to follow their dreams and fulfill their purpose. When I look back, it occurred to me, that God had altered my comfortable environment with some adversity, for me to find my purpose and walk into my destiny. The journey has not been easy, but it has been rewarding. I fell forward into my purpose. Had I stayed in bed; I would still be in bed!

Now that I have begun a new journey, these next few chapters are filled with information on my struggles and what I have learned from them. I am sharing these experiences because I want every woman who reads this book to know, that we have all experienced some challenges. However, through mentorship, coaching, and personal forgiveness, we can overcome our issues and fall forward into our purpose. By the time you finish reading this book, you will be empowered to write your own. Let us begin by taking control of the situation.

In order to walk into your purpose, we must all begin the journey by taking control over our lives. We can take the first step, when we accept the responsibility that we can alter our journey, even in the midst of adversity. Through my personal journey, I noticed that women struggled to move ahead because of the fear of prior mistakes. They are also afraid of what other people will say about their new direction, progress, or the changes they are making. The important lesson in this example is to understand that everyone makes mistakes. We are all works in progress, striving for perfection. A mistake is nothing more than a fall. Our goal is to learn from our mistakes and fall forward.

Also, when you take control over your life, you set yourself free from the embarrassment associated with the mistakes and experiences of the past. This freedom is also associated with forgiveness, and it opens the door towards accepting possibilities associated with your future. Another favorite scripture of mine states, "For God has not given us a spirit of fear, but of power, and of love and of a sound mind" (2 Timothy 1:7). As you take control over your life, focus on the fears you have about success. Know that you have the power within you to start over, and only you stand in the way of achieving success.

As women, one of the things we constantly ask ourselves is, how do we take control? The first step in taking control of your life is facing your fear. Fear hinders us from believing in dreams, ambitions, and possibilities. Instead of moving forward, individuals remain in their comfort zones. However, remaining in your comfort zone allows you to hide and ignore what is holding you back from success. To move forward, we often have to go back in time, and identify the fear, so we can find a solution and move forward.

Now, to help you move forward, let us go back in time, and think about some of the scariest things you have experienced and how you got through them. Do you remember your first kiss, your first date, your first job interview, your first airplane flight? Do you remember your first taste of rejection? In each case, there was probably a fear of failure or the fear of a bad outcome. However, you stepped up to the challenge, and moved forward. It did not kill you, and you managed to get through it.

Well, I want you to know, I experienced the same fear myself. For years, I have had a fear of heights in open spaces. I always believed I did not have enough protection. Last year while we were on vacation, my husband asked me if I would go zip lining with him. Well, for those of you unfamiliar with this outdoor adventure, zip lining involves the participant flying through the air, legs dangling, attached to a chord, which slides along a long cable.

Well, my first response to his request was a resounding no! However, I realized that the fear of heights was holding me back. It was robbing me of the possibility of a new adventure. So, I told my husband to pay the fee, and I would suit up. I just had to conquer this fear. While I was putting my helmet on, I am having this conversation with myself, believing that I am out of my mind. All geared up, we set out toward the takeoff platform. As I was walking up the steps, I was telling myself, it is not too late to turn back. I would be flying a total distance of about 780 feet, before landing on the opposite platform, which was about 30 feet above the lawn below.

While I was experiencing this "green mile," a little boy was walking up the stairs ahead of me. He could not have been any more than 6 years old. He had a big smile on his face, and he was so excited to take this ride with his brother. I do not believe he weighed more than 40 pounds, soaking wet. He moved forward up the steps, and seemed to have no fear whatsoever. I said to myself, "If he was zip lining, then so was I." I was not going to be out done by this cute little kid.

As I walked up to the rail, I could not believe I was going through with this. The instructor gave me the final instructions, told me to count to three, and step off the ledge. As I stepped off the ledge, it was like falling. However, in retrospect, I was falling forward. I realized that I was flying through the air and immediately the fear disappeared. I was gliding through the air with the wind in my hair, above the trees, looking at the lake, nature, and the people below. I realized it was no big deal, and that I could do it again. I had taken control of something that seemed overwhelming, and had haunted me for years. I look forward to enjoying that experience the next time we vacation at this resort.

Take a moment to list some fearful things that are holding you back. After you identify these obstacles, list the action steps you will take to move forward.

Obstacles:

_____

_____

_____

Action steps:

_____

_____

_____

Remember, fear robs us of possibilities and new experiences. Fear is the thief that comes to steal our joy and motivation. And fear is the enemy that comes to deter our progress, stifle our creativity, and destroy our dreams. When we face our fears, we negate the power that it holds over us. Today is the day to take control, face your fears, overcome by faith, and fall forward into your destiny.

TWO
Forgive Yourself and Learn from Your Mistakes

As we continue to live on earth, we will make some mistakes. We will encounter hurts, and often spend a lot of our time thinking about the issue. I want to talk to you about a variety of mistakes that you may have experienced. It is possible, that you may have cheated on a spouse, destroyed your marriage, engaged in questionable business ventures, betrayed a close friend, forgotten an important event, took advantage of someone, or have taken family members for granted. We have all done things we wish we could forget.

The problem with living in the past is that, it haunts us and keeps us from moving forward. We walk around carrying this guilt, and do not realize that it is holding us back. Guilt can often be the cause of stress, both emotional and physical. If you allow it to go unchecked, you may have unknowingly created heart disease, digestive issues, or anxiety disorders. Guilt can also change how we view ourselves and is often the source of a negative outlook on life. Plainly put, guilt will keep you from walking into your purpose.

When I think about it, guilt is often associated with how we react to life's events and our unhappiness with the outcome. As individuals, we often focus on our response, or the responses of others. We focus our attention on how we reacted, instead of focusing on the issue itself. Therefore, I want to challenge you to forgive yourself, document your mistakes, and move forward.

Now, you are saying to yourself, "Regina, that is easier said than done." Well, my new friend, you can, you shall, and you will overcome these issues. The first place to start is by forgiving yourself, and acknowledging your guilt. Understand that if you fail to do this, the issue will still haunt you.

Think about your daily routine. Do you focus mainly on negative things of your past? Have you failed to engage in new relationships because of a bad experience? Are you afraid to start a new business because of a prior business failure? Notice, if you fail to forgive yourself and move forward, it will rob you of a purpose-filled life.

Let me share an experience with you, so you can really see how guilt can control your life. All throughout my childhood, I maintained a relationship with a close friend. However, after we grew up and became adults, we both, kind of, went our own separate ways. I found out later that she blamed me for our split. In my mind, I had nothing to do with the split and had nothing to be ashamed of. However, I continued to carry the issue with me. Why was she blaming me for our split? We both started to date other people, went away to college etc. I would get married and start a new life. However, this past failed relationship would always remain an issue with me.

Years later, I ran into this individual. We talked, and I thought I had put the experience behind me. However, as time went on, I continued to have these private conversations with myself, where I continued to go back and forth on who was to blame. This issue would haunt me for years, and like most people, I was still carrying around the guilt of a failed friendship.

As I continued to hold conversations with myself, I began to focus on our relationship, and I realized that I had done nothing wrong. We had both been guilty of moving on and not maintaining our friendship. Once I came to grips with this, I received my freedom. I realized that my mistake was carrying around the guilt for both of us, and believing it was my sole responsibility for maintaining our relationship.

As I continued to analyze the issue, the bottom line became clear. We drifted apart, and we both failed the relationship. After coming to this conclusion, it was only one thing left for me to do, forgive myself and move forward. As I began to relieve myself of the guilt that I had carried for so many years, my life began to move forward in a positive way. I began to excel in other areas of my life, and the experience helped me learn how to manage issues better.

Now that I have shared that memory, I want you to take some time and focus on some of the mistakes you have made in the past. Maybe your issue was a past relationship, failed marriage or a bad decision. One of the best ways to deal with problems or issues is to identify those areas that haunt you in your private thoughts. I find that using a journal provides the best opportunity for self-expression and examination.

In a journal, I could list events, issues, or people that seem to haunt my past and were often the focal point for my guilt. A journal also provided me the opportunity to disconnect from the voice in my head, because the voice is now written on a piece of paper. I also found that I could also just write freely and list whatever was on my mind. Now, let's take some time to identify those feelings, by writing them below.

A. Hurt feelings that cause guilt.

_____

_____

_____

Now that you have listed some events, people, and issues that have been the focal point of your guilt. It is now time to identify what you have learned from these experiences. In the story I shared, I learned that I made myself the "gate keeper" of the relationship. However, we were both responsible for maintaining our relationship. Somewhere in the relationship, we failed each other. Once I was able to come to grips with that issue, I was able to forgive myself and I found the strength I needed to move forward.

I also learned through this process, that by forgiving myself, I removed the guilt and the power that it held over my life. It was also important for me to realize that everyone makes mistakes. Most importantly, I want you to know, that because you have experienced failure, that it does not make you a bad person. Remember, failure does not define you. The most important issue here is to learn from your mistakes and move forward.

Now, take a moment to identify what you have learned from your mistakes or disappointments.

B. Lessons learned

_____

_____

_____

Finally, if you want to forgive yourself and move on in life, we must learn to change our thought patterns. If you can change your thought patterns, then you can avoid dwelling on people, issues and events that create guilty feelings. You can create goals based on what you have experienced.

In order to move forward, you must view the issue from a different perspective. In my example of guilt, I focused on my actions. I failed to look at the entire situation, and thus, blamed myself for the outcome. In order for you to move forward, first pause and review the entire situation. Then document what you have learned, and forgive yourself.

Another key lesson regarding forgiveness is learning that the trials we face happen for a reason. We must also learn to believe that there is light at the end of your tunnel. Know that you may encounter other fears, or feel guilty regarding an issue. However, it is also important to know that how you manage these issues will determine your success.

Finally, as we end this chapter, I encourage you to create an action plan using these four steps. First, acknowledge the issue. Second, realize why you are in this place. Third, change your mindset by not focusing on your reaction, or the reactions of others. Instead, control your emotions and focus on the entire situation. Finally, take action to remove the guilt, find healing, and move forward.

THREE
Define Your Value – What are you Worth?

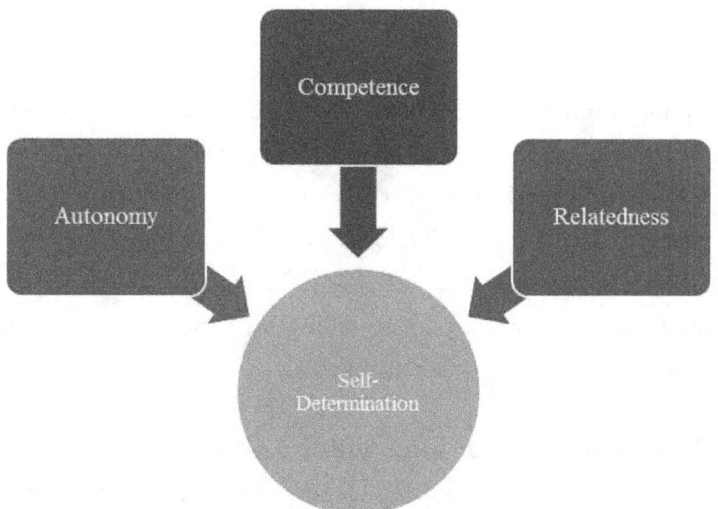

Have you ever watched a woman walk into a room, full of confidence, personality, and elegance, and you said quietly to yourself, "How does she do that"? Likewise, have you attended a business conference and watched a female speaker captivate a room, utilizing her individual skills to enthrall everyone listening to her every word? Both examples demonstrate women confident in their abilities and able to use their boldness, character, confidence, and unique style as part of their tools for success. In short, they are directing their own life, living by their own rules.

The same combination of personal assets provided in the examples above, are part of the tools you must use to define your value, and determine your worth. As you and I work through this chapter, we will focus on several key tools for success. These tools will allow you to reevaluate yourself, in order to help you understand your value and your worth. When you understand your value, you are on the correct path to falling into your purpose. The tools I have used to help myself grow are as follows:

- **Understanding your value and self-worth**
- **Understanding that I am a leader, and defining my leadership skills**
- **Improving my personal development**
- **Recognizing my own potential**

For women, understanding our value is critical in how we find the confidence to ask for a promotion, raise, or the corner office. For women who work inside the home, understanding your value is critical to how you help your husband and children. It is important for you to understanding that what you contribute is the glue that holds your family together.

What I have found on my journey of self-discovery is that value starts with a belief in yourself. I realize that sometimes as women, we undermine ourselves, thus placing a low value on our skills and abilities. If you do not believe in yourself, who will? When you believe in yourself, you are able to articulate and communicate your values and skills to key decision makers. Instead of walking away from the negotiation table, you are ready to negotiate from a position of power. The difference in negotiating from a position of power is your belief that you can turn that no, into a yes. I watched women on television promoting their goods or services, talking about policy issues, and displaying confidence. These women learned to use their voice, brains, words, and style to establish their value.

Therefore, remember that when determining your value, realize that it applies to your career, family, marriage, and self-esteem. If you do not demand what you are worth, you will miss the opportunity to learn what you are made of. You will also miss the opportunity to learn how you solve problems, and ultimately use your skills and attributes to define your success. Finally, it is critical that you understand your value, so that you can now help other women discover theirs. Remember the journey is not about you, but the individuals you will help along the way.

Take a moment and identify some of the most outstanding qualities that you possess, that define your value and worth. **Start each sentence with the words, I am...**

_____

_____

_____

Leadership

The second tool in the arsenal that I want to talk about is, leadership. Leadership is the ability to influence the relationship among leaders and collaborators, who desire to implement real change, inspiring others to act. For many years, female leaders have been balancing the stigma of traditional female norms, with male recognized norms, associated with leadership. As I evaluate my own life and worth, I believe women found the strength to walk away from traditional female stereotypes. This strength allowed them to start their own businesses, become news anchors, professional golfers, Senators, etc. However, women who exhibit strong personalities are often unfairly targeted, and viewed as too aggressive. If they are passive or overly careful while making decisions, it is seen as, weakness. Female leaders also struggle with an unevenly set bar, compared to their male counterparts, and often receive lower rewards for their efforts.

In addition, female leaders sometimes struggle with an identity crisis associated with their brand of leadership, and can spend countless hours asking themselves several questions. How can I gain respect from my peers? Should I wear a dress to work? Is my hair the right color? Should I dress like a man? Can I wear something else to work besides black, navy or gray? Are high heels acceptable in the boardroom?

Today, we have many female leaders serving in Congress. In the House of Representatives, some current female leaders include Maxine Waters, Barbara Lee and Nancy Pelosi, who served as the first female Speaker of the House. In the U.S. Senate, we have Amy Klobuchar, Debbie Stabenow, Kamala Harris, and Diane Feinstein. As I looked at state Governorships, we had Jenifer Granholm, in Michigan, and Christine Gregorie, in Washington. We currently have Gretchen Whitmer, Governor State of Michigan, Michelle Lujan Grisham, Governor State of New Mexico and Kim Reynolds, Governor State of Iowa. We had Loretta Lynch, serving as the first African American Female Attorney General and former Secretary of State Hilary Clinton, who ran for President of the United States.

When I examined the business community, I found a large diversity of women running major Fortune 500 Companies. Melinda Gates, founder of the Bill and Melinda Gates Foundation. Donna Langley, President of Universal Pictures. Ursula Burns, former CEO of Xerox and currently CEO of VEON. Rosalind Brewer has achieved great success as the former President and CEO of Sam's Club and currently COO of Starbucks. Finally, Michelle Buck, CEO of the Hershey Company.

When examining entrepreneurs, we have several women that have used their creativity and passion, demonstrating the importance of following your dreams. Sara Blakely is the founder of Spanx, promoting shape wear for women. Tory Burch is the founder and CEO of Tory Burch, of the ballet flat. J.K. Rowlings, Founder of the Harry Potter Empire. Cher Wang is the founder of the HTC Smartphone, creating opportunities for women in the technology industry. We also have Oprah Winfrey, who is constantly exploring new opportunities for women. Finally, we have you, the emerging female leader reading this book.

I have just provided a list of some incredible women. This group of female leaders are ethnically diverse, have different attributes, and share different views on issues affecting society. They represent a great example of women who have created their own path to female leadership, often stepping outside their comfort zones and defining their own values, thus determining their own self-worth. Their success can be used as inspiration, inspiring you to follow your dreams.

Now, I know I have just named some women who seem out of your league. Women you believe are far from your reach. However, I want you to realize that you are in their league. If you are a hockey mom, soccer mom, or homemaker, you are a leader. Your job may be without pay, but you get up and run a household every day. You challenge your troops to clean their rooms and do their homework. You are active in their education, manage the weekly transportation to games, and you encourage your team to stay focused and committed to their goals.

If you are a single mother, you are leading your family, by defying the odds that you are doomed for failure. You might be going to school and working two jobs, just to keep your lights on and pay the rent. My message to you is, do not quit! Stay focused, and remember that your short-term sacrifice is temporary. With hard work and dedication, you will soon see a light at the end of your tunnel. You are also providing the greatest example for your family. The lesson you are providing is that with a purpose and vision, you are unstoppable. You may experience some pain on this journey, but in the end, your testimony will lead others to victory. Be assured, that God is in control.

FALL FORWARD

For I know the plans I have for you, declares the LORD, plans to prosper you and not to harm you, plans to give you hope and a future.

Jeramiah 29:11

Through this process, I learned a lot about my leadership traits. I learned that I was self-driven, value based, compassionate, stylish, authentic, inspiring and goal oriented. Now, let's pause for a moment and have you identify your leadership traits. Start by looking back at my leadership traits, now list your own. **Start with the words, I am...**

_____

_____

_____

As I continue to work on my leadership skills, I have learned that it is important for us to define our leadership skill sets. This is why I would like to share some information with you that I have learned from other female leaders. Understanding your skill sets help leaders remain confident and bold. It also supports their ability to lead others. As we lead others, we are also working on improving our own leadership skills and abilities. As you look through this list, determine how many of these skill sets you currently possess, or will possess in the near future.

- **Do you share your success with others?** As female leaders, it is important that we build each other up. By sharing our success story, which includes our struggles, we can encourage others to find their own success. We can also use our talents to help others that believe they have no hope.

- **Are you a team player?** Young men learn the importance of teamwork, playing team sports. They learn that the entire team wins the game, and everyone associated with the team plays an important role. For women, we learn the opposite lesson from an early age, and often focus our attention on competing against each other. As female leaders, we must know how to take the negativity of competing against each other, and turn that into female leadership development.

- **Are you mentoring and developing your successor?** I have learned through experience, that the greatest contribution of a leader is their interest in developing others. Winning companies continue to thrive, when they invest in the development of their future leaders.

- **Can you develop mutual purposes?** In the business community, building mutual relationships can lead to success. If you have a new product you want to sell, someone working in your organization might have a solution to your problem. Yet this person may need more support or a pay raise. On the other hand, a colleague in another field may have a connection to someone that can help move your product or service to the next level, yet they may need your help in advancing their career. Can you bridge the gap and create an opportunity for both parties to benefit?

- **Do you value the gifts and diversity of others?** Examine your inner circle. Is it diverse? Does it challenge and encourage your development? Also, if you are the smartest person in your group, it is time to expand your inner circle. The knowledge and experiences of others can enrich your life. One way to accomplish this task is by joining professional organizations or volunteering your time.

- **Do you take risks?** As a leader, do you take risks or do you follow the same path daily. Do you give up because it is hard, or do you press forward? Are you afraid of succeeding, or afraid of failure? Examine how many times you heard the word no, before you heard the word yes. The fact that you pressed forward until you got to your yes, is validation of your commitment to succeed.

- **Do you allow for conflict among collaborators?** One of the key strengths of a leader is to be able to allow your subordinates to engage in conflicts in order to find common ground. Great ideas come from healthy debate. This can also be used as a team building strategy.

- **Do you encourage others in your organization or community?** Examine your organization and /or community. How many individuals are you encouraging to follow their dreams and passions? How much time do you spend helping others achieve their success? Are you volunteering your time to mentor young teens, or single mothers, to follow their dreams?

- **Do you advocate for the greater good?** Female leaders should be socially supportive and speak out for those who have no voice. There is growing evidence that when women wield power and assert themselves on the behalf of others, they do so effectively and without incurring repercussions. Women advocating for themselves are often seen as violating feminine gender norms, and both men and women alike, punish this norm-violating behavior.

All of us, whether we work inside the home, own our own business, or have an executive office, are leaders. Our followers are co-workers, members of our church, our neighbors and our family members. Our followers are counting on our leadership. Therefore, do not be afraid to walk into your purpose. Understand that sometimes you have to "fall forward" into your purpose, in order to, ultimately succeed.

Personal Development

The third tool in the arsenal that I want you to focus on is your personal development. Personal development is a process we can use to develop our skills and identify our talents, so we can design a pathway for success. Personal development can include a change in careers, higher education, and volunteer work. Personal development is also the opening for improvements in self-esteem, positive thinking, goal setting, and the backbone for a fulfilling life.

For many women, it starts with a clear sense of purpose and understanding of your self-worth. A sense of purpose can be found in a new career, raising a family, earning an education or spending time doing something worthwhile. When you have a sense of purpose, you know why you are getting out of bed in the morning. You find that you can smile, even during adversity. You understand that your purpose is greater than, yourself. This feeling leads to confidence, gratitude and a discovery of your self-worth. When you gain this confidence, you learn how to demand respect in the workplace. You feel comfortable about wearing high heels, taking charge in stressful situations, and finally pushing yourself to the limit.

One of the first keys to creating a personal development plan is, to ask yourself several questions. Your answer to these questions will help you determine how you feel about yourself.

- **Are you mastering life, or is it mastering you?**
- **Do you feel empty or dissatisfied with your life?**
- **How often do you try something new or different?**
- **Do you feel confident in yourself, or are you unsure?**
- **Do you walk with your head held high, or down toward the floor?**
- **While in a room of people that you do not know, do you speak first?**

As you reflect on the above questions, you may realize that you do not like the answers. The good news is that I have been in your position, and if I pressed my way through, so can you. The key is, taking it one-step at a time. You also have to realize that you deserve more, and you must be willing to do whatever it takes to achieve it. I know you may be afraid, but you have the strength down on the inside to overcome this challenge.

Therefore, I want you to review the following personal development plan. This plan is designed to help you learn more about yourself. You will list your goals, your challenges, and determine where you want to be. After reviewing this plan, and then creating your own, you will see a new road map emerging. This road map will help you define where you are, what you want, and the changes that will be needed for you to grow and achieve your goals.

Personal Development Plan

SECTION 1 – IDENTIFY GOALS		
Area for improvement	Where am I now?	Where do I want to be ideally? (No time limit).
Career	1. Dead end job 2. No challenge 3. Dislike being told what to do 4. Too many hours 5. Small salary	1. Career with purpose & passion 2. Challenge and adventure 3. Be my own boss 4. Work-life balance 5. Six figure salary
SECTION 2 - PRIORITIZE GOALS		
Career	1. Work-life balance, which leads to... 2. Challenge and adventure - because you have time to pursue something else like... 3. Career with purpose & passion, which can lead to... 4. Being my own boss, which can lead to... 5. Six figure salary 6. Higher Education, which leads to....	
SECTION 3 - ACTION STEPS (Based on your priorities)		
Career	To start finding work-life balance: 1. Find a way to carve out a few hours a week for my personal life – rather than just working all the time – even if it's reading a motivational book on the commuter train or bus, instead of working - (OR) 2. Take a walk at lunch time to give myself time to contemplate what I want out of life- (OR)	

	3. Journal at lunch time - (OR)
	4. Make one "self-date" a week to help me re-connect with what's important to me - (OR)
	5. Turn off the media and quiet my life down so I can go deep within and identify where I want to be.
SECTION 4 - TIME LINE FOR YOUR FIRST ACTION	
Career	1. Next week, I'll give myself two hours for just "me time "so I start feeling like I deserve something better- (OR)
	2. Tomorrow I'll buy myself flowers - (OR)
	3. Tonight, I'll send myself a message to start the process of feeling like I deserve something better.
SECTION 5 - WHAT WILL HAPPEN IF I DO NOTHING?	
Career	1. I'll be stuck in this dead-end job, day after day, never making progress or getting the life that I want.
	2. I may not start my new business.
	3. I may not have the child I want.
	4. I may not graduate from college.
	5. I may not receive the position I am qualified for.

When you can define your worth, you have now mastered the last tool in your tool belt. You now recognize your own potential, and with that, you have now created your own path. You have developed the formula to find courage in the face of adversity, understand your ability to solve problems, set goals that are authentic to your deepest desires, take risks, and build relationships that strengthen your purpose and vision.

When you have a plan in place, regardless to whether you are a stay-at-home mom, president, waitress, bank teller, CEO or grandmother, you feel confident about your abilities, and are willing to follow your own plan. You are now in the driver's seat, and whether you take a mountaintop view to the top, or country road, the choice is now yours.

FOUR
Find your Passion

Have you ever evaluated your definition of the word passion? When I first really began to focus on the word, I thought the word described something I like doing on a regular basis. However, when I used that definition, it covered many different things. For example, I love to read, play golf, go shopping, go to the hair salon etc. I enjoy all those things, but I was never passionate about any of them.

Passion wakes you up before daybreak, and the thought of that thing, issue, or event keeps you excited and engaged. Passion can also create a quieter feeling of satisfaction, knowing you are living life by your own design. Passion, when you attach it to your goals and dreams, becomes the fuel that keeps your fire burning all day long.

The challenge is often identifying what you are passionate about and moving forward towards that goal.

I realize that determining what you are passionate about is tough and can take time. It starts with how you define the word passion. When I talk to individuals, they talk about living a passionate life, but rarely focus on what makes them feel passionate. I want you to take a moment and think about your definition of the word passion. I believe that in order to live your passionate life, you must know the focus of your passions and how that connects to your passionate life.

Passion for me entails feeling excited to be alive, aiming for higher heights, helping others achieve education, encouraging people to use their God given talent, and enjoying special moments with family and friends. It is earning my own education, and watching others discover their unique purpose. It is writing this book, and hoping that you will discover that it is time for you to change your mindset and follow your passion.

As I began to think about my own life, I discovered that my passion for living evolved over time. I learned that I was not passionate about becoming rich, although I wanted to live a great life. Focusing on being rich was too much work, and required too much time. I believe that if you focus on your skills, use your gifts and talents, your wealth will follow. You may be asking me how that is possible? By utilizing your gifts and talents, you will find the passion you desire to start your own business, work in the sales industry, write books, promote your music CD, etc. The use of your gifts and talents will lead to your success.

For example, I have always desired to own my own business. I sold cosmetics, made soap, and operated a tax business. When I was selling cosmetics, I was happy holding parties and making women feel good about themselves. I would marvel at the amount of revenue that I earned helping to lift someone's self-esteem. It was not until I decided to move up through the company's sales promotion program that my interest changed.

My focus was now on getting women to join the operation in order to earn a commission. I would accomplish my goals, but I realized that what I had loved about the business was now secondary. I stayed in the business for several years because I had friends who were also part of the sales organization, and if they could do it, so could I. I had unfortunately bought into the trap of conforming to society's wishes, as oppose to following my own. That was my first mistake, because now my focus was not on helping women, but competing and keeping up appearances for others.

In this process, I became a different person. I saw women as possible paychecks. An opportunity that may have been a good choice for them, was now tainted by my own self-driven ambition. I became frustrated with operating a business controlled by someone else's rules. I wanted a business where I made all the decisions. I wanted this business to reflect how I wanted to impact society. I became uninspired, wearing myself thin trying to keep up with society's version of success.

One year, while attending the company's annual sales event, I was looking at my team and realized I was doing them a disservice. I was participating in a business concept that was a good business opportunity for some people, but not for me. I knew it was time for me to make a change. If I did not make a change, then my values and self-worth would be lowered because I was not following my true passions. I was living by someone else's standards and rules.

Eventually, I started a screen-printing and embroidery business. Today, I still own that businesses and I have received a lot of joy helping others with family reunions and business pursuits. However, it was not until I developed a good relationship with myself, that I realized my true passion was centered on my ability to help others achieve their goals. I began this journey obtaining higher education, co-authoring motivational books, and creating an organization, to help others find their own success. I stopped living according to the expectation of others, and created my own personal roadmap and my own definition of success.

As I took that first step, my desire to try new opportunities emerged. I joined professional networks and began to market my new business opportunity. I found that I was satisfied with my new direction and I looked forward to seeing where it would take me. Over the years now, it has become clear that my passion is geared towards helping others discover their unique gifts and talents. I find that I love to run into individuals, and hear that based on my instruction, they are excited to go back to school, have discovered a new career, have stepped outside their comfort zone, and are ready to take on the world.

I have shared this story because part of finding your passion centers on understanding who you really are, what you want, and what makes you happy. It also centers around, focusing on what you want to do with your life. Therefore, I want to ask you several questions.

- **What do you want out of life?**
- **What gets you excited?**
- **What are you good at naturally?**
- **How hard are you willing to work?**
- **Is your happiness worth the investment?**
- **Are you ready to walk into your purpose?**

I believe that when you can truly answer these questions, you can define what sparks your passion. Now take a moment and identify some things that ignite your passion. Try starting with the words,

I am really passionate about…

_____

_____

_____

Now that you have identified items that ignite your passion, how can you use those passions to help motivate yourself and others?

As I conclude this chapter, you must believe that passion and drive are within each of us. The challenge is to step outside your comfort zone, and be willing to embrace your passions and obtain a fulfilling life. Changing your mindset and view of your abilities, allows you to embrace every opportunity. As you continue to ponder this opportunity, know that fear is always present. You must always remember that you possess the tools that will give you the courage to succeed. You will never know how successful your journey will be, until you start.

FIVE
Change your mindset with Positive Affirmations

S o you have spent a great deal of your life being a pessimist, and you have learned to live with it. Let's face it, no one really helped you to see how being a positive person provided any benefits. You are waiting to see, what is in it for you. Well, my dear friend, being a positive person leads to positive results.

As an African American woman, I have faced many trials that challenged my belief in myself. Over time, I learned that it was the power of words that would help me overcome these issues. Growing up in the late 70s was tough. As a child I remembered that my parents were working hard to make a life for our family. My uncle had just come back from Vietnam. We had moved into a new house, and my father was trying to give us a better life.

For a child, it seemed like there were many things going on in the world that did not make sense. Black and white people were working on living together. Moreover, there was a large disparity between the have, and the have-nots. However, I was facing a new type of prejudice. It seemed that my own race was embroiled in a struggle between light and dark-skinned African Americans.

I remember my mom talking about her childhood, being separated from her other brothers and sisters, and living with her aunt. She encouraged us not to be afraid to embrace our heritage and to be proud of who we were. I remember going to grade school and someone telling me that I was as dark as the shoes I was wearing. I came home crying, and my mother told me that I was a beautiful girl and I had nothing to be ashamed of. I would struggle with this issue through elementary and middle school.

When it was time for me to go to high school, my mother enrolled me in Cass Technical High School. To my amazement, my classmates were Caucasian, African American, Hispanic, Asian, etc. The diversity was outstanding. As I embarked upon this new experience, my self-esteem lifted. I fell in love with the idea that color did not matter. We were all people, and as I embraced this school experience, I knew I wanted to live in a world where color did not matter.

As I mentioned earlier, I was fighting against what I believed were church rules created by men, for women. For example, we could not wear jewelry, pants, makeup, or shoes with the toes out. Why? Women were encouraged to get married, as oppose to going away to college, starting a business, traveling, etc. Somehow, I knew early in my young life that this was not the path I would choose. I wanted something different.

As I entered my young adult years, I felt great about myself. I was working, making new friends, and going on with my life. I also continued to push back on church rules. I was tired of hearing about what women could and could not do. I realized that I was breaking away and becoming my own person. However, the motivation I needed was still missing, and I could not understand what I was looking for.

Years later, I realized I was missing positive affirmations, and a positive thinking mindset, that I could use daily to describe myself to others. Creating a positive mindset is one of the most powerful life changing strategies anyone can use. The power of positive thinking, visualization, and affirmations can motivate you to achieve whatever you believe is possible.

When you think about it, positive affirmations are part of developing a powerful mindset. Professionals in all industries use these techniques to develop personal power or gain a competitive edge. At a personal level, it will transform your life, your health, and renew your joy and passion for living. Can you imagine waking up every day bursting with excitement, energy and joy, ready to start your day?

I know you are reading this chapter, and you are saying to yourself, "Regina, I do not believe you." Well, what do you have to lose? Try it out for yourself. **Listed below are some of the benefits of using Positive Affirmations.**

- **Positive affirmations** can help you develop a powerful and positive attitude towards life, which is an essential element for success and good health. This change in your mindset will allow you the opportunity to turn your failures into successes.

- **Positive affirmations** can aid in reducing depression. People who use positive affirmations know how to spin bad news into something positive. They realize they may be experiencing a crisis, but they do not lose hope.

- **Positive affirmations** can aid in creating a better psychological and emotional being because the person can cope with stress. By using positive thinking, I have learned to create a positive mindset to remove sadness from situations.

- **Positive affirmations can lengthen your life span.** When you engage in a positive mindset, you will have a positive outlook on life. You are willing to fight for what you believe in, and your activities will bear the fruit. For example, you will find the time to exercise, change your diet, and engage in activities that provide light versus darkness.

- **Positive affirmations allow you to share your positive outlook with others.** People will want to be around you because you are free from negative thinking. The wisdom from your experiences can be shared with others. Co-workers, family members, and peers, will look at your attitude and desire to learn more about why you are who you are? This allows you the opportunity to share your story, show your faith, and promote your gifts and talents, while encouraging others.

Finally, creating the right positive mindset allows you to tear down the mental walls that separate you from embracing new opportunities. The right mindset will allow you to see that your life matters, you provide value, and you deserve to move forward. The right mindset allows you to walk away from a bad relationship, because you understand you deserve more. The right mindset allows you the opportunity to stand in front of a mirror, and see value in yourself. Finally, the right mindset allows you to fall forward into your purpose.

I was able to use positive affirmations, and change my mindset, by changing the words I used to describe myself. I used these words to free myself from church rules, to embrace my African American heritage, and finally, to encourage other women like you to believe in yourself.

> **You are your worst enemy. It is your negative thoughts that hold you back, nothing else. Let go of the negativity, and life will change**

Therefore, I want you to erase these negative thoughts from your mind

- I am ugly
- I do not have any talent
- I am not qualified
- I will not succeed
- I am not pretty enough
- I have no friends
- No one loves me
- I will not graduate

I want you to find words that empower, celebrate, and support who you are. **Listed below are affirmations that I use daily for motivation and inspiration.**

- I am brilliant
- I excite others with my gifts and talents
- I am confident in my abilities
- I am determined to succeed
- I am committed to my purpose and passions
- I am focused on helping others reach their destiny
- I love life
- I am a warrior
- I am a conqueror
- I am a child of God

Throughout my journey, I have learned the importance of having a positive outlook on life. When faced with adversity of any kind, I know that through my faith in God, belief in myself, and the power of words, I can change any situation. I want to end this chapter with a passage of scripture that I believe connects to the power of using affirmations. It is Proverbs 23:7.

"For as a man thinketh in his heart, so is he."

Every time I read this passage of scripture and think about positive affirmations, I realize that what you say will become what you think. And what you think, ultimately becomes what you are. Therefore, use positive words to establish a proper positive mindset, and then fall in love with the new you that it creates.

SIX
Embrace Life - Mind, Body, & Spirit

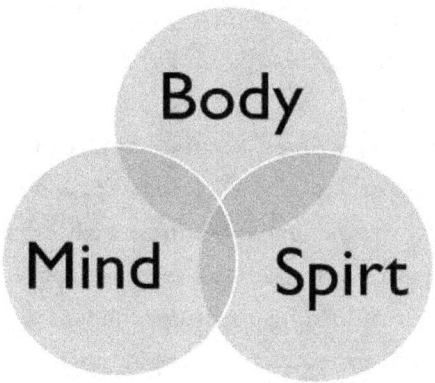

Your Mind

Do you struggle with being disconnected from yourself? Do you want to feel whole and display the best version of yourself? Do you talk about balance, but never seem to achieve it? In this chapter, I want to focus on you, and how you can transform your mind, body and spirit.

Years ago, I had the chance to attend a training offered by the Professional Woman Network. At this seminar, I earned my certification as a Holistic Life Coach, focusing on the mind, body and spirit. I chose this certification because I believe as women, how we talk to ourselves, treat ourselves, and view ourselves is the message we send to others. Our message will be positive or negative and connects to our individual view of our self-worth, abilities, and the respect we believe we deserve.

Well, when you look at the mind, body and spirit, it starts with our mind. Your mind is the link between your body and your spirit. The mind allows you to create perceptions of reality that produce a response towards a stimulus shared with your body, and is received in your spirit. If you have never thought about your mind, I want you to know it is a powerful tool. The mind can command the body to act, and those actions will affect both people and circumstances.

For example, a positive person will attract positive energies, and a negative person the opposite. Okay ladies, let me give you an example that you can recognize. Your cell phone rings, it's a family member, friend or co-worker. They never have anything positive to say, and you know that after you hang up the phone, your motivation is gone for the day. What do you do? You refuse to talk to that person.

One of the benefits of having a positive mind is being able to navigate through the negativity of others, while holding onto yourself. Without having a positive mind, your mind is now left cluttered with that information, and now you must work hard not to focus on the negativity. It is important that you create a process for unloading negativity, and protecting yourself from others. To do this effectively, you have to begin to work on your own mind.

First, maintain a self-awareness of your own strengths and weaknesses, and constantly look at how you can improve yourself. Knowing your strengths and weaknesses are important, but you want to always look at how you can channel your strengths, and turn weaknesses into positives. Second, keep a journal or recorder on hand. Journaling can help you clarify your feelings and thoughts.

For me, I truly began to connect with myself when I started to put my thoughts on paper. I learned to not just write down what I was doing, but why I was doing it. This allowed me the opportunity to go back and review my thoughts. I was able to review my emotions, and responses, and ask myself some questions. Am I too emotional? Did I overreact? Am I focused on myself? And most importantly, do I owe someone an apology?

Another tool I have found useful in dealing with my mind, is having a conversation with myself. In holding this conversation, I can ask myself about my plans, my relationship with my husband, friends and co-workers. I can ask myself about how I spend money, and how I pay my bills. Finally, by having a conversation with myself, I can remind myself about what I have learned from my past, so I do not make the same mistakes again. I encourage you to try it, and write in your journal what you have learned about yourself.

Another important area when protecting my mind is being aware of my image. Sometimes what we believe about ourselves is different from how others view us. I agree that we should not live by other people's opinions, but deep down we know if people have a positive or negative view of us. If people think of you as strong, are you using your strength to empower others? If people have a negative view of you, this provides a great opportunity for self-awareness and correction.

When you focus your mind on something relevant, you can achieve whatever you desire. When we think positively about ourselves, we set the tone for how we will live. You may fall many times through the process, but deep down, you know you are falling forward into your purpose.

Your Body

Your body connects to your spirit because it has to be respected and taken care of. When you think about it, it is true. Having a yearly physical, eye exam, breast exam, or dentist appointment, reduces your risk of disease. Now ask yourself, and be honest, do you really take the proper care for your body? Do you drink too much alcohol? Are you allowing workplace stress to cause you to overeat? Are you avoiding exercise? Are you getting enough sleep? And finally, how is your diet?

Well if you have just read the above paragraph, as I did, you are shaking in your boots. I read that paragraph and gave myself a grade. I had to think about what I was doing. Every day, I make a smoothie with Kale, Spinach, Fruit and Juice. I exercise and I eat a salad for lunch. However, am I doing enough? The answer is no. Next month, I will start a yoga class because I have determined that this year I will reduce my stress and take on new experiences.

Therefore, I have listed some helpful suggestions designed to help us all improve. If you are going to lead others, change the world, and walk into your purpose, we must change how we care for our bodies. Please review the list, and ask yourself the following questions. After some reflection, write the information down in your journal.

1. Are you eating fresh fruits and vegetables?
2. Are you drinking enough water?
3. Are you getting enough exercise?
4. Are you getting enough sleep?
5. Are you engaging in some outside activities, such as bike riding, golf, swimming or horseback riding? If not, add some of these to your list this year. You will be surprised how much fun you can have.

When you start to incorporate these ideas into your daily routine, you will begin to see some positive results in your overall health.

Your Spirit

Your spirit is the component of a human person, where people focus the least amount of attention. Your spirit is your guide to the deeper meanings of your human experiences. It teaches you to learn from your own mistakes, and helps guide you through life. The key for your spirit is maintaining a certain level of balance. Balance for your spirit requires that you understand love, overcome fear, embrace forgiveness, and use wisdom.

I have just listed four important attributes associated to your spirit. Love allows you to embrace harmony in your body, mind, emotions and spirit. It allows you to walk towards a path that provides joy and inspiration. It allows you to love others, and be loved by others. Overcoming fear allows you the freedom to pursue your passions and express your God given creativity. Forgiveness is tough because you must let go of pain. When you forgive someone who has hurt you, you let go of those negative feelings that have you bound. Forgiveness allows you to embrace life, as you free yourself from the bondage of past hurts and disappointments.

Wisdom is something we develop as we mature. Your own experiences all contribute to your wisdom, whether they are positive or negative. The lessons you have learned, play an essential role in the development of your wisdom. Therefore, understand that the lessons you have learned, and the wisdom you have gained, are what you will ultimately use to help others. Finally, as you continue to grow and learn, you will be capable of handling life's challenges, based on your own wisdom and experience.

The mind, body and spirit, are connected and rely on each other for success. Remember to understand that your mind, body and spirit, function as one. Clear your mind of negative thoughts, and focus on a path for success. Execute your plans, reflect on your experiences, and use the wisdom gained to feed your mind with good thoughts. When you do, good things will follow.

SEVEN
You are a Virtuous Woman

A wife of noble character who can find?
She is worth far more than rubies.
Her husband has full confidence in her
and lacks nothing of value.
She brings him good, not harm,
all the days of her life.
She selects wool and flax
and works with eager hands.
She is like the merchant ships,
bringing her food from afar.
She gets up while it is still night;
she provides food for her family
and portions for her female servants.
She considers a field and buys it;
out of her earnings she plants a vineyard.

She sets about her work vigorously;
her arms are strong for her tasks.
She sees that her trading is profitable,
and her lamp does not go out at night.
In her hand she holds the distaff
and grasps the spindle with her fingers.
She opens her arms to the poor
and extends her hands to the needy.
When it snows, she has no fear for her household;
for all of them are clothed in scarlet.
She makes coverings for her bed;
she is clothed in fine linen and purple.
Her husband is respected at the city gate,
where he takes his seat among the elders of the land.
She makes linen garments and sells them,
and supplies the merchants with sashes.
She is clothed with strength and dignity;
she can laugh at the days to come.
She speaks with wisdom,
and faithful instruction is on her tongue.
She watches over the affairs of her household
and does not eat the bread of idleness.
Her children arise and call her blessed;
her husband also, and he praises her:
"Many women do noble things,
but you surpass them all."
Charm is deceptive, and beauty is fleeting;
but a woman who fears the LORD is to be praised.
Honor her for all that her hands have done,
and let her works bring her praise at the city gate.

Well, I have just listed a bible passage about the Proverbs 31 Woman. After reading this passage, some of you may have said to yourself, who is this woman? Well the truth of the matter is we are all, in some way, the virtuous woman. Let me explain.

The virtuous woman in this passage is a woman of noble character. She is a hard worker, taking care of her family and friends. Her children speak well of her. Her husband also finds her praiseworthy. When she conducts business with the merchants, she is considered a trustworthy soul. She is full of wisdom, and shares it with those she cares about. Finally, she is a woman of strength and a woman who knows that with God, all things are possible.

Now, I want to talk about you and how you can connect yourself to the virtuous woman. In today's environment, women play a variety of roles. Some of us are homemakers, while others work outside the home. Today, some of you are school Principals, Senators, Pastors, Worship leaders, Business executives, Administrators, Business owners, Mothers, Godmothers, Aunts, Grandmothers and sometimes you play the role of a Father, if the dad is absent. Your duties are never ending and your family looks to you for guidance and support.

The interesting thing I love about the virtuous woman is that she represents every woman, regardless of race, size or financial status. For example, if you are a mom, you are working hard to provide food for your family. Your children see you as a woman of strength and dignity. You are up late at night, working to make sure your children lack nothing. Your skills are so strong that you can run a household, PTA meeting and soccer club, at the same time. In addition, you are the doctor, the cook and the lawyer. You are everything!

As a single mom, whether it was your choice or someone else's, it is all on you. You are the nurse, the father and the coach. You are the breadwinner and the decision maker. You sometimes have to hold two jobs to make it work, but you are up for the task. You may often go without a coat to make sure that your children do not suffer. As the passage states, you are not afraid of the snow. This means that even during your darkest hour, you will still rise to the occasion in order to guarantee your household's survival.

If you are married, and a modern woman, you are extremely challenged to maintain a household, marriage and career. You are often the glue that holds everything together. You are setting an example by showing other woman that having a family, career, and love is possible. As a wife and career professional, you use your earnings wisely to support your family. In the above passage, she buys a field with her earnings. Well, for many of you who are planning a future for your children, this would be a similar investment.

To the corporate CEO, the writer, the educator, and the small business owner, your husband finds value in what you bring to the table. In addition, because you are a virtuous woman, you do not use your position to belittle his manhood. You handle yourself with grace and dignity, befitting a woman of virtue. The important thing to remember is to conduct yourself with honor and dignity, and your family will consider you blessed. They will also recognize that, by you being blessed, they are blessed as well.

For the grandmother who is dedicated to raising her grandchildren, your unconditional love is part of what keeps the family together. You have made this choice because you realize the importance of family. Through your leadership, you are setting the example for those who shall follow you, protecting your legacy. You are in charge of the neighborhood block club and the family reunion. You are viewed as the matriarch of your family. Your words, your life and your strength, have set the tone for how everyone will live. Family members, friends and others, sit at your feet to hear your words of wisdom, and glean from your knowledge.

For the woman on the road to recovery. You have survived domestic abuse, drug abuse, alcoholism and possibly rape. Your journey has been a long road to recovery. You may have dropped out of high school, and now you are on your way to earning a bachelor's degree. You survived living in shelters, and now you live in your own apartment or have your sights on home ownership. You have changed the statistical data, by not becoming a statistic. Through your road to recovery, your story is powerful, because you had to rely on your faith and trust in God to get you through. You fell so many times, you did not think it was possible to get up. However, you fell right into your purpose.

For the widow, you are now starting over. Depending on your circumstances, you are now the leader of the family. You are now challenged with beginning a new life without your partner. You are now focused on taking over the household, and recovering from your loss. As a virtuous woman, you are now honoring the memory of the one you loved, who is no longer with you. Your mind is racing with thoughts. You are possibly asking yourself, what am I going to do? How can I start over, and why did this happen to me? Know that this event in your life is part of your journey, and once you recover, it will serve as a story you will share to encourage others. Remember, God will not put more on you, than you can bear.

Now, I want to talk about myself. As I read that passage, I realized that all the things I have experienced are part of my journey. In order to fall into my purpose, I had to overcome racism, hatred, inequity, and control by others. I had to find words that empowered me to walk into my purpose. I had to find friends and mentors, that could speak life into my situation. I also had to learn the importance of being myself, and creating my own path.

For example, I had to start a business, and learn that there was more to life than money. I learned that wealth is important, because it allows you to take care of your family, support your church and plan for your future. However, through my struggles, I was reminded that I was blessed when I gave to others, knowing that it was God that would supply all of my needs. I have survived business failures, and have been unemployed. However, I used those particular experiences to earn higher education, and learn that my purpose and strength lies in encouraging and helping others.

This final chapter represents the journey you and I have experienced. The purpose of sharing the passage about the virtuous woman is to let you know, that we are all virtuous women. We work, we take care of our family, we take care of others. We have survived abuse, unemployment, adversity, and pain. In the end, our faith pulls us through.

Our failures are part of our journey. Without them, we could not boldly fall into our purpose. Failing to start a business, by a house, receive a promotion, simply means it is not your time. Therefore, understand that while you are experiencing this valley, you are learning about yourself, your strengths, your weaknesses, and your ability to succeed. Always remember that the next time you experience a challenge, or any failure, that you are falling forward into your purpose.

Now that you have read the final chapter in this book, I want you to look in the mirror and know that you are a virtuous woman. Your failures are part of your journey. Keep your faith in God and believe in yourself. With this, you will accomplish whatever you desire.

Oh, and about that question that I always wanted answered as a child. Why some of us were born to struggle, while it seems others were destined for prosperity and success? Through my experience falling forward, I learned that life is much like a game of cards. When the cards are dealt, you have no control over the cards that you receive, or the hand (circumstances / opportunities) that it forms. Seeing that we have no control over this process, we have only one responsibility. With all of our heart, mind, determination and ability, we must play the hand that we were dealt. Moreover, we must play to win. In life, you can only give your very best effort, and trust God to make up the difference.

Finally, I learned not to compare myself to others. Their cards are their cards, and the cards that I have been dealt, are mine. When God created me, he created me to follow the path that he has laid out for me. That path is uniquely, tailor made, just for me. In the end, I trust that He knows best. When I learned to embrace this fact, I found peace, and fell forward into my purpose.

Dr. Regina Banks-Hall

Resources

Executive Presence for Women - Coni Masciave
What Are You Worth – Natalyn O. Lewis
Interior pictures courtesy of Pixabay and Canva

About the Author

Dr. Regina Banks-Hall is the founder and CEO of RBH Professional Development Institute, an organization focused on helping individuals and organizations through professional development, leadership training, and coaching. RBH Professional Development Institute conducts workshops, mastermind classes, seminars, keynote presentations, and lunch and learns, for corporations and individuals.

Some of the workshops include: Leadership development, team building, mastermind classes on personal growth, vision boards, teen leadership, women in leadership and small business startups.

RBH Professional Development also provides publishing services. RBH Professional Publishing, a division of RBH Professional Development Institute, helps firms and individuals promote their books and periodicals, through all major publishing channels.

Dr. Banks-Hall is also the owner of Regina's All-Star Apparel &

Accessories, an online promotional product company. Regina's All-Star Apparel & Accessories helps organizations utilize promotional products for marketing, advertising, team building, and customer appreciation.

Dr. Regina Banks-Hall is also a College Professor, who instructs university students in the areas of business, leadership, and economics. Some of her courses include Small Business Administration, Leadership Theories, Change Management, Economics, Marketing Management and Human Resources Management. Dr. Banks-Hall received a Bachelor of Business Administration in business management and a Master of Business Administration in Human Resources Management from Baker College. Dr. Banks-Hall earned her Doctorate in Business Administration from Walden University, with a concentration in Leadership.

Dr. Regina Banks-Hall is a gifted motivational speaker, professor, mentor, and coach. She is very active in her local community, working in a handful of positions in her local church, while also mentoring both young men and women. She is a certified Holistic Life Coach, through the Professional Woman Network and is a certified Independent Teacher, Trainer, Coach, and Speaker with the John Maxwell Team. Dr. Banks-Hall has served as an Advisory Board Member for the Professional Women's Network, President and Area Director for a local Toastmasters Chapter, and Board Member for the Michigan Association for Female Entrepreneurs.

In addition, Dr. Regina is a member of the Society of Human Resources Management (SHRM), Association for Talent Development (ATD), National Association of Professional Women (NAPW), Golden Key International Honor Society, National Society of Leadership and Success (NSLS) American Management Association (AMA), Toastmasters International and the Michigan Association for Female Entrepreneurs (MAFE).

She is the co-author of several books: *The Confident Woman: Tapping Into Your Inner Power, The Female Leader: Empowerment, Confidence & Passion, Second Chance Living: Out of the Darkness, Into the Light* and the *International Female Leader*.

Dr. Regina believes her purpose in life is to inspire everyone to overcome their fear and walk into their destiny. To purchase books, journals or other promotional items, please visit www.rbankshall.com or www.regina-gifts.com. Also, please subscribe to her blog at www.drreginabankshall.blog and podcast show, "Maximize Your Life" with Dr. Regina Banks-Hall, wherever you receive your podcasts.

To book Dr. Regina Banks-Hall for workshops, seminars, keynote speaking, mastermind classes and publishing services please email regina@rbankshall.com. You can contact her by phone at (866) 600-6322 or by mail 2000 Town Center, Suite 1900, Southfield, MI 48075. Also, search for her on Facebook, Instagram, LinkedIn, Pinterest, YouTube and Twitter under her name, Dr. Regina Banks-Hall.

www.ingramcontent.com/pod-product-compliance
Lightning Source LLC
Chambersburg PA
CBHW052118070526
44584CB00017B/2539